COINS

TODTRI

A QUANTUM BOOK

Published in the United States by
TODTRI Book Publishers
254 West 31st Street
New York, NY 10001-2813
Fax: (212) 695-6984
E-mail: info@todtri.com

Visit us on the web!
www.todtri.com

ISBN 1-57717-214-0

QUMCCCN

This book is produced by
Quantum Publishing Ltd
6 Blundell Street
London N7 9BH

Printed in Singapore by Star Standard Industries (Pte) Ltd

CONTENTS

THE EARLY COINS

• • • •

BELOW Barter, swapping goods, was the original means of making payments before money. Then items such as strings of cowrie shells and gold came to represent the value of the goods.

Three-quarters of a century ago most transactions were made in coin, but the First World War saw gold replaced with paper money.

Now, the services that are offered at banks in our cashless society have become even more sophisticated; computers and improved electronic communication technology have combined to make the spending of money easier than it has ever been. Today all you need is a piece of "plastic" and you can travel the world with hardly any need to handle notes or coins.

Throughout history people have measured their wealth in many ways – herds of cattle, hides, land, gold bars, bonds and stock certificates, or a row of figures at the bottom of a bank statement. But none of these will buy you an ice cream or a loaf of bread. It is in the everyday business of life that coins come into their own.

Barter

Coins, as we know them, have been around for almost 3,000 years. Before that, and today in more remote regions of the world, money took the form of objects on which a value was placed. In the old civilizations of the pastoral Mediterranean basin wealth lay in sheep and cattle. On the hoof or slaughtered, these animals were used for barter and this is reflected in many words pertaining to money that are used to this day.

From the Latin *pecus*, meaning herd, we get the word "pecuniary". The Greek for cow-hide was *talanton* from which came the word "talent", meaning a specific weight, and therefore a specific value, of gold or silver. "Purse" and "bourse" (a place where money changes hands) are derived from *byrsa*, an alternate word for "cow-hide", while "salary" relates directly to the salt, paid as wages to Roman soldiers. The Latin *pondus*, meaning a weight, has given us "ponder" (to weigh up), "ponderous" (heavy) and, of course, "pound". Even the British pound symbol (£) comes from the Latin *libra*, denoting a specific weight of one pound.

Growing money

The saying "money doesn't grow on trees" suddenly takes on new significance when you consider that the Arabs once used beans, called *qirat* (from which came "carat" or "karat") as currency.

Agricultural produce has often been used as money in the past, in fact until the 1950s the inhabitants of Tristan da Cunha, a tiny island in the middle of the Atlantic Ocean, said that two potatoes equalled a penny.

Other natural products have also been used as money. Cowrie shells, *Cypraea moneta*, for example, were once used as small change in many parts of Asia and Africa.

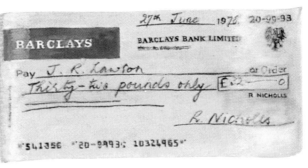

ABOVE AND LEFT
The progression from coins, which were in use in Asia Minor in around 650 BC, to credit cards, which were developed in the 1950s, takes in paper money and checks.

ABOVE *The Chinese li (or cash).*

ABOVE *The Japanese 200 mon coin.*

From objects to coins

Shell discs, wampum, glass beads, feathers, shark and walrus teeth, and even stone cartwheels have been used as money. But the development of coins really began when metal representations of objects replaced the real object. In Asia, bronze utensils that had been traded for centuries were substituted by bronze miniatures of the utensils.

Copper is probably the oldest metal to be used as money. Copper comes from the Greek *copros*, meaning dung, which gave Cyprus its name, because copper was mined there 5,000 years ago. Alloyed with tin found in Cornwall in England, it produced bronze. Small bronze axes, known as celts, were used as money in Gaul and Britain. The earliest Roman coinage consisted of lumps of rough bronze, called *aes rude*.

BELOW *A 50 tael piece of Sycee silver from China.*

In China, small discs of copper or bronze with a square hole in the middle began to evolve as coins long before the Christian era. The type was eventually fixed in 620 A.D. and remained current until the 1920s, making the Chinese *cash* the longest-used coin. However, it had little value and great numbers would have been required.

ABOVE *The Fe – a piece of primitive stone money from the Marshall Island.*

From 1644 to 1768 the Swedes made transactions using heavy and cumbersome copper coins — one giant measured an impressive 14in by 24in. The inconvenience of both China and Sweden's coins probably explains why they were the first countries to introduce paper money.

In other parts of the world where iron was more readily available, it was used as the raw material. In ancient Britain and Greece, crude bars or spits of iron were used as money, and in West Africa the *kissi* (a small, winged iron rod) was used until the beginning of the twentieth century.

RIGHT *The gold Oban of Japan carried the mintmaster's name on its ridged surface.*

Value marks

Metals as exchange media were well established in ancient Greece at least 1,000 years before the Christian era. Gold in a relatively pure state was not as popular or as practical as its alloy with silver, known as electrum or pale gold. Initially, merchants had to weigh each piece of electrum for every transaction. This was a time-consuming process, so it came about that the pieces of metal were given a mark that guaranteed weight and purity.

At first the mark that guaranteed the weight and quality of the metal took the form of a personal stamp, struck on the lump of metal with a broken nail whose jagged end would leave a distinctive impression. It is from this crude device that the chopmarks, which Chinese traders applied until recent times to silver coins imported from Europe and America, developed.

Through Europe and the Middle East, however, the mark of the individual merchant developed into a single device that eventually occupied the whole of one side of the piece of metal. At the same time the lumps of metal became flatter and rounder. By 630 B.C. the crude nail mark had developed into a recognizable motif. This was a lion's head, the badge of the Mermnad dynasty that ruled over Lydia in Asia Minor (modern Turkey). The motif was engraved into the face of an iron

anvil, and a lump of heat-softened electrum was placed over it. When it was struck forcibly by a hammer, the electrum would flatten and pick up the impression of the motif. The side bearing this motif is known as the obverse of a coin, or "heads".

RIGHT A scene from William Shakespeare's "The Merchant of Venice". Fifteenth century merchants were very powerful in northern Italy. Their innovations in coinage were widely copied in Europe.

Heads or tails?

At first the reverse, or "tails", was left blank and such coins are said to be uniface (one-sided). Gradually, it became the custom to engrave a mark on the hammerhead and later on a piece of iron, which produced a simple, geometric incuse (meaning, cut into the surface) pattern on the "tails" side of the coin.

Because the reverse took the force of the hammer-blows and the engraving wore more quickly, the important and enduring motifs were used on the obverse. The obverse dies that have survived from Roman and medieval times generally have a large spike on the back. This was driven into a block of wood that took the place of the anvil. The reverse die had a flattened back to take the hammer-blow.

The next stage was to make the reverse as elaborate as the obverse. The earliest coins of this type date from the middle of the sixth century B.C. and were minted in Athens. The obverse bore a profile of the goddess Athena, while the reverse depicted her attribute, the owl. This established a precedent that was followed by many of the Greek city-states: a portrait of a deity on the obverse and a pictorial emblem on the reverse. This pattern persists to this day, hence the effigy of Queen Elizabeth II on the obverse and the lion on the reverse of British coins, or the profile of George Washington linked to the American eagle on the American quarter dollar coin.

By the fourth century, the whole of the civilized world used coins, each kingdom, principality and city-state having its own distinctive series. Nowadays, there are not many countries without their own coins and none that does not use coins in one form or another.

ABOVE The obverse of the American quarter dollar shows George Washington, the first president.

ABOVE The reverse of the American quarter dollar with the bald eagle.

ABOVE The silver tetradrachms of ancient Athens bore an owl motif.

ABOVE This "owl" of Athens bears the inscription of the city name, ATHE.

CHAPTER ONE

MAKING COINS

• • • •

There are two methods of producing coins: casting and the die method. The die method is the one used to make modern currency.

Cast coins

The earliest coins of ancient Rome, the *aes rude*, and their successors, the *aes grave* (heavy bronze), were cast in molds bearing the shape or impression of the required casting. Casting was the technique used in China to produce the *pu*, *shu* and *tao* bronze pieces. The chi 'en, or *cash*, were also cast, often in clusters or "trees" in which individual coins were linked by branches created by the molten metal running through the channels of the mold. Complete trees are rare and much sought-after. You can recognize a cast coin by the marks on the edge showing where the tunnel has been broken off, or by the file marks where attempts have been made to smooth this away.

Japan's cast coinage commenced in 708 A.D., with copper, bronze, brass or iron, *mon*, and silver *chibu Gin* and gold *Nibu Kin* in use until 1870. The most spectacular were the gold and silver, large, thin, round-cornered *Koban*, *Goryoban* and *Oban* stamped with chops and inscribed with characters painted in Indian ink. Korea used cast coins from 1633 until 1891, some Malay States until 1895, and Indochina and Burma (who had previously used cast pieces in the shape of hats, cannon and animal figures) until the nineteenth century. Elsewhere, cast coins were fleetingly used, often in times of emergency.

BELOW The Isle of Man halfpenny of 1709, is a rare example of a cast coin from Europe.

FROM CAST TO COIN

LEFT Refining and smelting the gold.

LEFT The molten gold is poured into fire-resistant molds and cast into ingots prior to rolling into coinage strip.

Die method

This involves impressing the image from a die, or pair of dies, on a piece of metal by means of a hammer blow. The piece of metal, known as a blank, flan or planchet, was originally cast in a shallow mold. The Spaniards in Latin America cast raw silver into bars, sliced it to make blanks that were clipped to the right weight, then heated and hammered between two dies. The result was crude coins, versions of the famous pieces of eight, which are known as cobs, from the Spanish *cobo de barra*, meaning "cut from a bar".

The method developed in Europe in the Middle Ages was to hammer out a sheet of gold or silver to the required thickness and then cut out a circular blank with stout shears. The blanks were then trimmed and filed to the exact weight, and were struck by hand. The Greeks attained considerable skill in the cutting of dies and the resulting coins with their comparatively high obverse relief are masterpieces. Roman coins, on the other hand, are generally flatter, with much greater emphasis on the lettering of the legend or inscription.

The art of coining suffered during the Dark Ages. The techniques of intaglio gem-engraving, practiced by the Greeks and Romans, virtually disappeared. Medieval European coin-makers made little attempt at realistic portraiture and effigies became highly stylized. The lines of the images and legend were punched into the dies.

It was not until the Renaissance that the design and engraving of dies reached the standard attained by the Romans a thousand years earlier. From then until the early nineteenth century, the quality of coin design rested largely on the craftsmanship of the engraver. Each die was engraved separately, so that the coins of a single issue varied considerably .

In the 1820s, a number of technical advances were made. Collas of Paris invented a reducing machine that did away with the need for hand-engraving, and a chemical processes for hardening steel revolutionized the manufacture of dies.

Modern coin design

The design of a modern coin begins with an artist's pen and ink sketch. Experts including art historians, museum curators and representatives of the government consult to insure that the design is accurate. In the case of the United Kingdom and many Commonwealth countries, the monarch approves the design personally.

Once the design has been approved, an enlarged and detailed marquette is fashioned in Plasticine or modelling clay. Casts from the marquette are perfected with fine dental drills. The master cast is then made into a matrix of hard chrome and nickel and fitted to the cutting machine. The image is cut on a hub or master die by a steel cutter working in unison with a stylus that moves over the matrix.

The image is then transferred from the hub to the working die. A negative impression is picked up on the die, using a powerful press. The die is hardened by heating it in a salt bath, then quenching it in a special solution. This gives the die its intense clarity. Finally, it is ground and polished by hand, using diamonds.

BELOW Dies used to produce emergency copper and brass 20 heller coins in East Africa in 1916.

Mechanization

The coining strip was the first aspect of the coin making process to become mechanized when, in 1551, machinery was installed at the Moulins des Etuves in Paris to roll out the metal to a uniform thickness. Huguenot refugee Eloi Mestrell brought the technology to England and produced the first milled coins between 1561 and 1571. Nicholas Briot revived the notion, first at the Paris mint and then, from 1625, in England. Civil War interrupted Briot's work, but Pierre Blondeau under the patronage of Oliver Cromwell milled coins on wide release in England by about 1662.

Enormous coiled strips are delivered to the mint where they are cut into flans in blanking presses under a pressure of 50 tonnes per square inch. After cutting,

LEFT Sculpting the master design for a coin.

the blanks are checked, degreased, cleaned, washed, dried and then they are brought to a brilliant luster

Presses for making coins were devised in the fifteenth century. Donato Bramante (1444–1514) invented the screw press, but this was quickly superseded by the roller press, the dies of which were ovoid, not circular. Hand-operated devices were used well into the

nineteenth century until James Watt and Matthew Boulton produced coins on steam presses.

The celebrated Cartwheel twopence of 1797 being one of the first of its products. In 1818, Dietrich Uhlhorn invented the lever press and it settled in to universal use.

In modern high-speed presses, blanks are fed into the dial plates and checked for thickness and diameter, before reaching the coining station where they are struck. If a coin is overstruck while another coin is on the dial plate, collectors call it a brockage. A brockage may have imperfect and slightly doubled impressions.

Should the mechanism fail to put a blank on the dial plate, the dies strike each other leaving clash marks that then appear on subsequent blanks.

LEFT Craftsmen at work in a medieval mint.

CHAPTER TWO

WHAT IS IN A COIN?

• • • •

The coinage of a country is usually divided into categories according to the metals or alloys used. In the past the principal coinage metals were gold, silver and bronze (or copper) for which collectors use the abbreviations AV, AR and AE (from the Latin *aurum, argentum* and *aes*).

Gold

In historic times, gold coins were usually minted in almost pure metal of 23.5 carats fine. The modern equivalent is "three nines" gold (999 in 1000 parts) and these numerals may be found on such modern bullion coins as the Canadian maple leaf. In 1984, however, the Royal Canadian Mint succeeded in refining gold to .9999 pure, and began striking maple leaves with the "four nines" inscription. The drawback of pure gold is that it is very soft.

In England in 1526, King Henry VIII debased his gold by introducing the crown of the double rose, struck to only 22 carat (.917) fineness. Later English monarchs operated a dual system of "fine" gold (mainly for pre-sentation pieces) and "crown" gold (for everyday circulation). This continued until the outbreak of the Civil War in 1642, but thereafter only crown gold was used in coinage.

British gold was traditionally alloyed with copper – hence its reddish luster. In several countries gold is often alloyed with silver, resulting in a more yellow color.

ABOVE AND LEFT The "angel" was introduced by Edward IV in 1465 and was last minted by Charles I shortly before the outbreak of the English Civil War.

Silver

In its virtually pure state silver, like gold, is too soft for practical durability, yet this was the fineness that was used for the *pesos a ocho reales*, the famous "pieces of eight" that were produced in such abundance by the Latin American mints. In medieval Europe the purest silver obtainable was 23/24 or .958 fine, and was known as Königsilber or Argent le Roi (king silver), but it was rarely used for coins.

ABOVE AND RIGHT British farthings from the reign of queen Victoria were struck in copper (above) and bronze (right).

In England from Anglo-Saxon times, 92.5 per cent silver was alloyed with 7.5 per cent copper. This mix was used for the silver pennies or "easter-lings", from which came the term "sterling".

Henry VIII progressively debased his silver coinage ending with .333 fineness. Any alloy containing less than 50 per cent silver is known as billon. Henry's billon coins contained so much copper that they were nicknamed "Coppernoses".

The record for the poorest quality is held by Mexico whose pesos of 1957 to 1967 were a mere .100 fine!

Copper

Copper and the alloys derived from it have been widely used for coinage since classical times. It fell out of favor in Western Europe, although it continued to be used in the Byzantine Empire, and formed the basis of currencies in the Far East. It re-emerged as a coinage metal in Europe in the sixteenth century.

In England, when the public demanded copper farthings for small change, King James I granted a license in 1613 to mint such coins in copper, but it was not until 1672 that the government bowed to economic pressure and authorized base metal halfpence and farthings. Pure copper was used for British subsidiary coinage until 1860 when bronze was substituted.

ABOVE A pure nickel Dutch gulden.

BELOW The first US nickel five cent coin.

Bath metal, which contains a high proportion of zinc to copper, was used to produce the Irish halfpence, the Rosa Americana coinage (1722-4), and pennies for the Isle of Man in 1734. Bell metal (78 per cent copper and 22 per cent tin), from melting down church bells; and gunmetal (90 per cent copper and 10 per cent tin) were used for Irish coins struck by James II in 1689 to 1690.

ABOVE Stainless steel
Italian 100 lire.

Platinum

Platinum was used for Russian rouble coins from 1826 to 1845. In the 1960s countries, such as Sierra Leone and Tonga, produced platinum coins. In 1983 the Isle of Man launched the noble as the world's first bullion coin in this metal. Since 1966 palladium – a metal of the platinum group – coins have been struck.

Nickel

Nickel as a coinage metal languished between the third century B.C. and nineteenth century when it was added to copper to make the Flying Eagle cents (1856-8) and the Indian Head cents (1859-64). This alloy was subsequently adopted by the United States for three cent and five cent coins. The five cent continues and is known as the "nickel", but nickel was replaced by copper, silver and manganese from 1942-5. As a substitute for silver, pure nickel has since been used by many countries: Switzerland for the 20 rappen (1881), Austria for the 10 and 20 heller (1892), and nickel alloyed with steel has been used in recent years by Afghanistan.

BELOW Danish zinc
coin (1957).

Iron

Iron has been used extensively for 150 years. It was used for the cast 20 *cash* Hsien Feng coins of Fukien and Chekiang (1851-61) and in Doosa-Seni coinage of Japan. Iron coins appeared in various parts of nineteenth-century Africa. It was used in Europe during the First World War. Norway and Denmark produced coins in varnished iron, while Sweden used nickel-plated iron in 1917. A form of stainless steel known as acmonital has been used in Italy since 1939.

ABOVE A Polish zinc
ten groszy coin.

ABOVE A zinc
Austrian coin.

Zinc

Zinc coins were plentiful in Asia in the nineteenth century, and it was first used in Europe in Czechoslovakia (1923-5). During and after the Second War it was used in Nazi-occupied countries. War-time coinage of Canada used a zinc alloy. Zinc-coated steel replaced bronze in the American cent coins of 1943. Zinc/copper alloy is used for jiao coins of the People's Republic of China. A triple alloy is now widely used.

ABOVE A Belgian
zinc coin (1945).

Tin

Even though tin corrodes badly it was used for English farthings of 1684-92 and the halfpence of 1685-92, and Antiguan farthings of 1836. It was only in Malay for kepings and pitis that tin was used to any great extent.

Pewter (tin alloyed with lead) coins appeared in China, but otherwise tin was an emergency choice.

Potin (20 per cent silver mixed with copper, tin, zinc and lead) was favored by pre-Christian Celtic tribes with the addition of a little gold. A similar mixture was used for tetradrachms struck at Alexandria.

ABOVE
Aluminium coins from Poland and the People's Republic of China.

Lead

Lead in its more or less pure form was used by Frederick III of Denmark for several denominations minted in about 1660, and it was fleetingly used in China and the East Indies. Its most noteworthy use was in a series of coins issued by the Andhra dynasty of India between 100 B.C. and 200 A.D.

LEFT Aluminium coins from Iceland and Cyprus.

Aluminium

Aluminium made its coinage debut in 1907 when it was used for British West African tenth pennies and for British East Africa half cents. However, aluminium proved too insubstantial for the public's liking and in 1908 it was replaced by cupro-nickel. Several countries had emergency issues of aluminium tokens during the First World War. Between the wars, aluminium is found only in some coins struck in Germany and Romania, but the use of this inexpensive metal was widespread in small coins from 1938 onwards.

Alloyed with bronze, the heavier substance was first used by France for the Chamber of Commerce 50 centimes and the one and two francs of the 1920s. It was also used for East Germany's 20 pfennig coins, and for Germany's rentenpfennig and reichspfennig coin issues from 1923 onwards.

RIGHT Mexican 50 centavos issued in 1951 and made of aluminium-bronze.

FAR LEFT British West Africa pioneering aluminium tenth-penny of 1907 and (LEFT) a 1911 replacement made of cupro-nickel.

Alloys

The vast majority of coins are struck from an alloy in which the component metals are mixed at the molten stage. In classical and medieval times, base metal coins were sometimes given a "wash" of gold or silver to give them the appearance of precious metal, and there are numerous examples of coins of the present century that consist of one metal plated with another. Chrome-plated steel, for example, was used by France for five centime coins (1961-4) while the United States used zinc-plated steel for the cents of 1943.

Coins have also been made of two different metals or alloys. The main blank (the outer ring) is of one cheaper metal, but into this is set a plug or small disc of a more expensive metal. English farthings of 1684-5 were made of tin, but their value was enhanced by a copper plug. In recent years, Italy has issued 200 lire coins with a steel outer ring and an aluminium bronze center.

BELOW The bright golden color of the aluminium-bronze Vatican 20 lire (1981) depicting Pope John Paul II.

ABOVE Joseph Moore's bimetallic model penny.

21

Non-metallic coins

During and immediately after the First World War, several European countries permitted the circulation of pasteboard tokens, which may be found in square, octagonal or circular shapes. During the monetary crisis that overtook Germany immediately after the First World War, the Meissen potteries produced emergency coins made of porcelain or stoneware on behalf of several municipal authorities and chambers of commerce, for general circulation in 1921-2.

Thailand had porcelain coinage during the nineteenth century. These pieces were originally produced as gambling tokens, but during a shortage of small change they were pressed into service. In 1913, the Cocos (Keeling) Islands introduced a series of seven coins made of a proto-plastic substance known as ivorine. These were followed in 1968 by a series in colored plastic discs (blue for the cent denominations and red for the rupee values) that remained current until 1977 when more orthodox coins of bronze, cupro-nickel, silver and gold were released.

SHAPE

The earliest coins were irregular lumps of metal with a constant weight and fineness. Primitive coins took on globular forms (Lydia), bean-shapes (ancient Persia) or bullet-shapes (Thailand). The larins of the Persian Gulf States and Maldive Islands were thin bars of silver, stamped with the denomination, which were often bent at one end to resemble a fish hook. Still on a marine theme, the sycee currency of the Far East was boat-shaped. But possibly the most eccentrically-shaped were the silver wire dengi (a forerunner of the kopek) of the Russian principalities in the fourteenth and fifteenth centuries.

ABOVE Obverse of the Ceylonese square five cents (1971).

Many medieval coins are concave and scyphate (cup-shaped), and the best-known examples are the gold nomisma. Prince Frederick-Henry of Orange (1625-47) struck scyphate coins, *schusselheller*, that were uniface and concave.

Square coins

Square coins range from the copper Indo-Scythian examples of pre-Christian times to the Afghan aspers of the nineteenth century. Many German and Scandinavian states in the late medieval period struck square or lozenge coins, known as klippe or klipping.

ABOVE Square coin from Malaya, showing George VI.

In some cases, the dies for circular coins were merely struck on square flans, but in other instances special dies were employed, with ornaments occupying the spandrels. The spandrels being the spaces between the arc of the circle and the corners of the square. The Moghul emperor Jahangir (1605-27) issued round and square rupees in alternate months.

Modern square coins include the Sri Lankan five cent (1909-71), the Dutch five cent (1941), the Burmese ten pence (since 1952), the Philippines one cent (since 1975) and the Bangladesh five pence (1973-80). Poland struck klippe in bronze, silver and gold between 1933 and 1938.

In 1975 Colombia celebrated the tercentenary of Medellin with a gold 1000 pence coin in a square format.

Many Indian coins since 1942 have been square, but the alignment of the motifs means that a truer description is diamond-shaped. Other diamond-shaped coins are the Bahamian 15 cent (1966), and the Jersey ten shilling coin (1966), which celebrates the ninth century of Norman Conquest.

ABOVE The Japanese Isshu Gin (one shu silver) issued in the mid-nineteenth century.

BELOW A circular design struck on a diamond-shaped blank. This is the 1704 klippe of Ulm, Germany.

Triangular coins

Triangular coins, like the vast majority of four-sided coins, have rounded corners, and the biggest disadvantage is that they are unsuitable for coin-operated equipment as they do not roll.

The first coinage of Gabon (1883) included a ten centime with three truncated sides and a triangular 20 centime, both being cut from sheet zinc. In 1988, the Cook Islands introduced a series that included a three-sided, two dollar coin.

Many-sided coins

When it comes to coins anything from 5 to 12 sides is possible. Here is quick run down from pentagonal to dodecagonal: five-sided Belize $100 coin (1981); six-sided coins have heralded from Djibouti, Egypt and the British Virgin Islands; seven-sided United Kingdom 50 pence (1969), Falkland Islands, Barbados and Tonga; eight-sided heller from Augsburg (1744-76); ten-sided coins struck in Afghanistan (1979), Colombia (1967) and the Dominican Republic (1983); and 12-sided coins include Britain's 1937-67 threepence, Australia's 50 cent (since 1969), Botswana's two thebe (1981) and examples from Argentina, Chile, Cyprus and Fiji.

Wavy-edged coins

The wavy- or scalloped-edge device has found favor with many African and Oriental countries where a largely illiterate population can recognize the value of coins by their shape. The Moghul Empire probably holds the record for the most shapes used by a single country, with round, square, diamond, elliptical, triangular and rectangular coins, and this tradition has been maintained to some extent by modern India and Sri Lanka.

While Jersey had a 12-sided threepenny, like the United Kingdom, neighboring Guernsey preferred a coin with a scalloped edge.

Variations in the sides of coins are adopted when new values are added to a series and a different shape is preferable to increasing the size. Thus the United Kingdom avoided the need for a coin of five times the size and weight of the ten pence coin by issuing the heptagonal 50 pence. Hong Kong was forced to face the dilemma of already having quite a large dollar coin when it was decided, in 1975, to introduce a two dollar coin. The problem was solved by using a coin of much the same weight, but with a scalloped edge.

Coins with holes

Holed coins do not, as a rule, permit portrait or pictorial motifs, but Australia managed to achieve both in a very curious coin of 1988. This was, in fact, one of a pair of coins that celebrated the 175th anniversary of Australia's first distinctive coins – the "dump" and the "holey dollar".

In 1813 Lachlan Macquarie, Governor of New South Wales, having procured 40,000 Spanish dollars at 4s 9d each, ordered that their centers be cut out. The circulated centers, known as "dumps", were countermarked "fifteen pence", while the outer rings – the "holey dollars" – were countermarked with the name of the colony, the date and a new value of five shillings. The canny Australian governor thus made a profit of Is 6d on each Spanish dollar.

In the 1988 silver coins, the "holey dollar" had a face value of one dollar, whereas the corresponding dump was valued at 25 cents. The dump bore the profile of Queen Elizabeth on the obverse and Aboriginal figures on the reverse, but a tiny version of the Queen's profile appeared at the top of the "holey dollar", while the reverse bore an Aboriginal snake pattern draped around the hole.

Chinese *cash* and other cast coins of the Far East were produced with a square hole in the center so that they could be strung together. Usually strung as if stacked, some *cash* are strung in an overlapping pattern to form

"swords" or long rods. In the Western world where coins were struck rather than cast, a hole did not emerge until 1863 and only then after one million holed coins were minted in England for Hong Kong emulating the *cash* previously used in 1887. Paris struck bronze sapeques for French Indo-China with a square central hole.

Holed coins, and in some cases square holes, came to be linked with colonial coin issues or, as happened in Norway in 1921 and Denmark in 1924, to satisfy legal requirements of weight without sacrificing size.

ABOVE A bracteate of the south German States.

A holed coin can limit design, but not always. Albania's 50 leke coin (1988) commemorating the country's railway system, has an off-center hole simulating a tunnel out of which emerges a steam loco on one side and a modern diesel electric on the other.

Thickness

Because the earliest coins were struck from lumps of metal, they tended to be fairly thick with rounded edges and high relief. But from Roman times and through the Middle Age, coins became thinner. This was in part due to the fact that it was easier to cut blanks from well-hammered, thin plates. This was taken to extremes in the twelfth century in Thuringia where the blanks were so thin, almost paper-thin, that the impression of the die showed through on the other side in reverse. Known as bracteates, meaning "hollow pennies", they spread throughout the Germanic world and flourished for about 200 years.

The dicken (meaning "thick"), was a silver coin, minted in Berne in 1492, and it came to set the standard for large silver coins. But with the abundance of silver in the sixteenth century, and with the rolling machinery and screw press, it was expedient to produce heavier and thicker silver coins.

ABOVE Reverse of the first nickel-brass circulating coin (United Kingdom, 1983.)

RIGHT Prototypes for the Isle of Man thin (1978) and thick (1987) and Guernsey (1981).

26

The size and thickness of a coin did not just result from whimsy, but from legal need. The British copper twopence (1797), nicknamed the Cartwheel, had to be a certain size in order that it contained copper to the value of twopence. And once a coin is as large as is practical, the only remaining option is to make it thicker. Hence, the Cartwheel became the thickest British coin in circulation.

On 28 December 1335, the King of France signed a decree authorizing the issue of piéforts. These presentation coins were struck from normal dies, but using flans two or three times the usual thicknesses and weight. Though presentation coins were struck for dignitaries visiting the courts of Henry VII of England, King Philip II of Spain and Albert and Isabella in the Netherlands, it was in France that piéforts attained their greatest popularity, eventually being struck on a regular basis for sale to collectors even to this day.

LEFT United Kingdom five pence of 1971 and (BELOW) the later, smaller issue.

Size

The size of coins has varied enormously, both between coins of different value, as one might expect, and also between coins of the same face value. An excellent example of "shrinking" coinage was provided in June 1990 when Great Britain reduced the size of its five pence

BELOW Mexican pesos of 1963, 1978 and 1984 showing the reduction in size.

27

coins from about 0.9in to 0.75in, while retaining the design and alloy. This was quite a shock to the British public because the five pence, and its pre-decimal equivalent, the shilling, had remained the same since 1816.

RIGHT nineteenth century Columbian gold peso coin.

The British five pence did not shrink alone, there was also the Mexican peso that had a diameter of about 1.5in and contained .786 troy ounce of silver until 1914. When minting resumed in 1918, it had shrunk to 1.3in and the silver content was only .4663 troy ounce. The diameter remained constant until 1967, although the silver was progressively debased. In 1970 it emerged as a cupro-nickel coin with a further reduced diameter and plumetting real value. Since then it has fallen to less than a tenth of its previous value and the 100 peso coin (currently the smallest in circulation) is virtually worthless.

The smallest

In 1904 Panama introduced a 2½ centesimo coin of about .35in, weighing a mere 0.04oz. Popularly known as the "Panama pill" or "Panama pearl", it was reintroduced in 1975 and since then has been struck by the Royal Canadian Mint or the Franklin Mint of Philadelphia. Amazingly, though, this coin is a giant compared to small coins from other parts of the world.

In 1328, the Ottoman Empire introduced the akce, which contained 0.04oz of pure silver and had a diameter of a mere 0.3in.

But for tiny coins you have to look back to classical times. The Greek hemitetartemorion or eight odol, which would buy you a glass of wine in ancient Athens, was less than 0.1in across and correspondingly thin. Athenians kept these tiny coins – with ironically one of the longest names – safe by carrying them about in their mouths!

The record though for smallest coin goes to Roman billon or copper minim (from *minimus*, smallest) of the fourth and fifth centuries. These averaged 0.8-0.12in, but some *minimissimi* discovered from the Lydney Park hoard in 1929 were not much bigger than a pinhead.

The largest

The Cartwheel twopence of 1797 was cumbersome, but there have been even larger coins. The Roman *aes grave* coins, for example, included such monsters as the dupondius, quincussis and decussis, which weighed two, five and ten Roman pounds, respectively. In fact the decussis coin weighed in at a massive 6lb!

Large base-metal coins reflected the cheapness of copper compared to silver or gold, but some really large coins have been struck in precious metals.

The largest English gold coin ever produced was the triple unite struck at Shrewsbury and Oxford during the Civil War. These 60 shilling coins measured about 1.8in, but their weight was only 1oz.

The largest American gold coin was the $50 of 1915 that commemorated the Panama-Pacific Exposition. This coin weighed about 3oz and had a diameter of 1.6in.

But for the true giants, it is necessary to look elsewhere and back in time. The gold multiple mohurs of the Moghul Empire, issued by Emperor Jahangir in 1639. The 100 mohur had a diameter of about 3.8in and weighed about 4lb 10oz.

A 1,000 mohur, which were all thought to have been melted down, was found in 1987. This fantastic coin, which was minted at Agra in 1613, weighed 26.5lb and had a diameter of 8in.

The farthing

In bygone times, when coins possessed an intrinsic value equivalent or close to their face value, the size of coins reflected the everyday needs of the people.

In Tudor times even a farthing (a quarter of a penny) had real spending power. Because England – unlike many other European countries – took a pride in issuing even the humblest coins in a high silver standard, the usual practice was to cut a silver penny into four, made easier because of the cross on the reverse. Farthings as separate coins were struck from the time of Edward I onwards, but by the reign of Queen Elizabeth I the value of the farthing had dwindled to the point at which it was more trouble to mint than it was worth.

Because a farthing was still needed in small change, however, the Mint devised an ingenious solution to the problem. Silver pennies and halfpence continued to be struck as before, but a three-farthing coin was added to the series. Because these coins did not bear their actual denomination, it was necessary to distinguish between the new and the existing denominations. This was achieved by adding a rose to the obverse, behind the queen's head. This was alluded to by William Shakespeare in "King John":

"... my face so thin
That in mine ear I durst not stick a rose
Lest me should say, "Look, where threefarthings goes!"

LEFT One of the smallest English coins – the farthing.

The silver farthing, last minted the reign of King Edward VI, about 1551, had a diameter of only about .35in making it the smallest English coin.

ABOVE *The Indian rupee (1985) with the distinctive multi-sided frame.*

ABOVE *The two-franc coin of 1979 with a hexagonal frame.*

ABOVE *The circular Anthony dollar of the United States (1979) with a polygonal frame.*

Rims and edges

These terms may seem synonymous, but collectors distinguish between them. The rim is that part of the surface of a coin at its circumference; it is a line of raised metal – thick or thin, plain or beaded – running round the perimeter. It plays an important role in modern coins for it both protects the surfaces of the coin and helps in stacking. Stacking was not a matter that concerned the minters of hammered coins and it is virtually impossible to stack these one on top of the other without them falling over.

Within the thin rim of modern coins there is usually a ring of fine ornaments, either circular beads or elongated teeth. This is the kind of detail that tends to vary from one die to another, and collectors looking for minute variations are often reduced to painstakingly counting these beads or teeth.

The side of the coin viewed end on is described as the edge. In hammered coins, the edge was usually left plain, although a notable exception was Roman coins of the first and second centuries B.C. that appear to have nicked edges. It has been suggested that this serration was intended to show the purity of the metal or that as these coins were intended for circulation among the Celtic tribes, the serration echoed their ring amulets.

Milling and graining

The experimental milled coins of Eloi Mestrell and Nicholas Briot had plain edges, but great attention was paid to the regularity of the flans and the beaded rims. The beading of the rims would have deterred people from clipping off slivers of precious metal. In 1662, however, when milled coins were adopted in England on a

FAR LEFT Incuse
inscription on the
raised rim of an
Isle of Man silver
crown (1987).

LEFT The United
Kingdom
Cartwheel
twopence (1797).

permanent basis, added security was provided by adorning the edges with grooves running at right angles to the rim. This is often mistakenly referred to as milling, but the correct term is graining.

Some coins have been recorded with a fine or coarse grain, and counting the notches provides the variety searchers with more work. The interrupted grain found on the 50 cent coins of New Zealand and the pound coins of the Isle of Man assist blind people to distinguish between coins.

When graining takes the form of short lines set at an angle to the rim, it is known as a cable edge. The Hong Kong five dollar has an edge with close beading contained in a sandwich of thicker, horizontal lines. Also in use is an edge of floral or geometric ornaments in relief.

RIGHT "Sandwich" edge and (FAR RIGHT) "interrupted graining" edge.

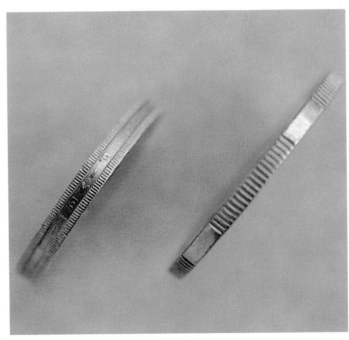

Inscriptions

Another very popular form of edge decoration consists of inscriptions. These appeared on the larger coins of Charles II when milling was adopted in 1662. These coins bore the Latin inscription *Decus et Tutamen Anno Regni* followed by a numeral. The inscription was not only ornamental, but also deterred people from clipping the edge. When the British pound coin was introduced in 1983, the Royal Mint revived this motto, inscribing it incuse in addition to vertical graining.

BELOW A rare instance of a coin showing the day, month and year of issue.

As a rule, edge graining and inscriptions are confined to circular coins. Coins with a scalloped or polygonal edge are usually plain-edged, but a notable exception was provided by the Isle of Man, which issued a seven-sided, 50 pence coin in 1979 for the Manx Millennium Viking Voyage. Subsequently, these coins were reissued with an incuse inscription round the edge: H.M. / Q.E. II / ROYAL /VISIT / I.O.M. / JULY / 1979. (Slashes indicate that each part of the inscription occupied on of the seven sides.)

Because the inscription was applied after the coins had been struck, it was impossible to insure that the inscription began at the same point on each coin or that the coins were obverse-up or -down at the time of striking. As a consequence, there are 14 collectable varieties of this coin to be found.

How coins are inscribed

Edge ornament and inscriptions are usually added to coins after the obverse and reverse have been struck, using a rocking bar with the ornament on a strip of steel resembling a spring. Alternatively, the collar that surrounds the blank can be engraved with the desired ornament.

When the coin is struck, the immense pressure causes the metal to flow and fill the grooves and recesses of the dies. The metal will also fill any spaces that are left within the collar.

ISLE OF MAN · FIFTY PENCE ·
DAY OF TYNWALD
JULY 5th

PROOF AND COMMEMORATIVE
COINS AND TOKENS

● ● ● ●

Not all coins are intended for everyday use. The definitive is a permanent issue designed for general circulation. There are also proof or sample coins, commemorative coins and tokens made to celebrate an event. These by-products of coin making have always been much sought after by collectors.

Essays and proofs

Sometimes a design will actually get as far as the engraving of dies, but the issue may not proceed. Pieces struck from these dies are regarded as essays, trial pieces or patterns. In some cases, the differences between essays and the issued coins are very slight. As a rule, essays are rare because only a handful may have been struck.

Trial strikes to test the dies, are known as proofs. Originally, proofs were often pulled on a metal, often lead, other than that intended for the issued coins. Because proofs were struck one at a time they were of better quality than mass-produced coins.

In the eighteenth and nineteenth centuries, proofs were often struck and presented to visiting officials and government ministers. Out of this charming custom arose the notion of producing proof sets for sale to collectors. Proof coins can usually be distinguished by their superior finish and that a precious, rather than base, metal has been used. Coins minted in metals other than those in general circulation are said to be off-metal strikes (OMS). A "diamond finish", "library" or "specimen" describes a proof coin struck in a base metal, but given a superior finish.

BELOW Proof set of New Zealand coins (1982) including the silver version of the Takahe dollar.

DOLLAR IN EVERYONE'S LANGUAGE

In 1519, the Counts of Schlick began striking large silver guldengroschen. They could afford to do so because their silver mines at Joachimsthal in Bohemia (now Jachymov in Czechoslovakia) were among the richest in Europe. These beautiful large coins were nicknamed Joachimsthalers, but this was soon shortened to "thaler". The term was applied to any large silver coin and it spread to other countries, which modified the

word to suit their own languages. Thus it became a *talar* in Saxony, a *tallero* in Italy, a *talari* in Ethiopia and a *tala* in Samoa. In Denmark, however, it became a *daler* and in Holland a *daalder*, while in English it eventually emerged as a dollar. This name was applied to the Spanish *peso de a ocho reales* – the "pieces of eight" associated with the pirates and buccaneers of the Spanish Main.

BELOW Samoan tala coin.

ABOVE Macau's 100 pataca coin.

ABOVE Bermuda crown (1964).

LEFT Canada dollar.

RIGHT Hawaiian one dala coin.

BELOW LEFT New Zealand dollar.

BELOW Dollar-sized coin for the 1992 Olympics.

BELOW RIGHT Another Olympic coin issue.

Commemoratives

Commemorative coins date back to 510 B.C. when Elis began striking coins for the four-yearly Olympic Games. Many of the so-called "large brass" of the Roman Empire celebrated a victory, the inauguration of some public building or an event of great importance.

In the Middle Ages, when coins were quite utilitarian, there was little inclination to use them to celebrate an event, although English silver pennies of the late tenth century that depicted the Lamb of God, may have marked the millennium of Christianity.

The Holy Roman Empire

While the Spanish dollars tended to stick to the same motifs, with the heraldic interpretation of the Pillars of Hercules (Straits of Gibraltar) and the Latin motto *Plus Ultra* (more beyond, meaning America), the *thalers* issued by the kingdoms, duchies, free cities, margravates and bishoprics of the Holy Roman Empire and its neighbors vied with each other in their imaginative motifs to mark royal birthdays, weddings and coronations. Mourning *thalers*, for example, bore a portrait of the departed on one side and the royal successor on the other.

The United States

The United States began issuing commemorative coins in 1892, when a half dollar celebrated the quatercentenary of the discovery of America by Columbus. This was reissued in 1893 with a quarter-dollar honoring Queen Isabella of Spain.

Considering the popularity of silver dollars in general, it seems strange that until very recently only one commemorative silver dollar was issued, to commemorate the Marquis le Lafayette (1900). It was not until the 1983 Los Angeles Olympic Games that silver dollars were again used for commemorative purposes.

The preferred medium for American commemorative coins was the silver half dollar, of which 46 different types were minted up to 1954. Interest waned because it was felt that these coins had been overdone, and no further commemoratives were issued until 1976 with a set of three coins — quarter, half dollar and dollar — to celebrate the bicentenary of Independence. Since 1982 there has been a resumption of commemorative half dollars and higher denominations, reflecting a relaxation in the law that permits citizens to possess gold coins.

LEFT Silver proof with frosted relief on a mirror table of the Canadian Winter Olympic $20 coin (1985).

The United Kingdom

The United Kingdom has pursued a very conservative policy with regard to commemoratives. The silver crown of five shillings was the ideal medium for this, beginning with the Silver Jubilee of 1935. Subsequent crowns celebrated the Festival of Britain, the Coronation (1953) and Sir Winston Churchill (1965). Decimalized as 25 new pence, crowns were issued to mark the Silver Wedding (1972), the Silver Jubilee (1977), the 80th birthday of the Queen Mother (1980) and the marriage of the Prince and Princess of Wales (1981). When the crown was next issued in 1990, it was revalued as a five pound coin and issued to celebrate the Queen Mother's 90th birthday.

Meanwhile, the United Kingdom has flirted with a commemorative 50 pence coin to mark entry into the European Community in 1973, and two coins for the Commonwealth Games and the tercentenaries of the Bill of Rights and the Claim of Right (both 1988).

LEFT The reverse
of the United
Kingdom two
pound coin
marking the
Commonwealth
Games, Edinburgh.

Base-metal commemoratives

Not by any means are all commemoratives large, expensive coins in silver or gold. In recent years, many countries have issued base-metal circulating coins to publicize the "Food for All" campaign of the United Nations Food and Agricultural Organization, although in many cases off-metal precious versions and proofs were also released.

One could form a very interesting, yet quite inexpensive, collection devoted to base-metal commemora-tives. Canada, for example, has had several coins of this type, ranging from the bicentenary of the nickel indus-try nickel (1951) to the centenary of the Mounties quarter (1973).

FAR LEFT The Canadian quarter to mark the centenary of the Mounties (1973) and (LEFT) Thailand "Food for All" base-metal commemorative.

Tokens

Nowadays all coins are mere tokens, with little or no intrinsic value. In practice, however, the term "token" is reserved for subsidiary coinage that is not authorized by the government. Tokens are not legal tender in the sense of coins, but they serve the same purpose as coins with perhaps no more than local validity.

The Stuart monarchs made a half-hearted attempt to supply base-metal halfpence and farthings from 1672 onwards, but only after 4,000 merchants and shopkeepers had issued lead, copper, brass, tin or pewter farthings in the period before the Great Fire of 1666. A failure of the government to issue copper halfpence and farthings after 1775 led to a revival of tokens (produced in an astounding range by a variety of businesses and traders with motifs of landmarks and even advertizing) that ended in 1797 when the Cartwheel coinage was introduced. Tokens enjoyed another revival during the Napoleonic wars when there was a shortage of silver.

Many of the earliest coins of Australia, Canada, Ireland, the Isle of Man and Gibraltar resulted from the initiative of local merchants and bankers. In the United States there was the so-called "Hard time" tokens (1834-44) and those carrying advertizing and patriotic motifs produced by shopkeepers during the Civil War.

Tokens known as trade dollars are currently extremely popular in Canada where they are issued to celebrate local events and given a limited period of validity. Many other kinds of tokens, while not actually valid as coins, have or once had a monetary value representing goods or services, or are encashable for coin of the realm. Into this category fall everything from transportation tokens to gambling chips. Shopkeepers have given tokens to customers, redeemable on purchases at a later date. These are all highly collectable and are of particular interest to the local collector.

ABOVE Obverse of the brass Canadian Hudson Bay Company token.

ABOVE "Ships, Colonies and Commerce" halfpenny token.

ABOVE Reverse of the Hudson Bay Company token.

LEFT Bath penny trade token of the eighteenth century.

CHAPTER FOUR

PORTRAITS AND PICTORIALISM, MARKS AND SYMBOLS

• • • •

The vast majority of collectors concentrate on amassing coins according to the country of issue and the subjects depicted on them. Some define their collection even further by focusing on inscriptions, cryptic marks and symbols.

Portraiture

In ancient Greece, the portrait of a god or goddess usually featured on the obverse, and an attribute on the reverse. But upon the death of Alexander the Great, who was regarded as a god, his portrait began to appear on the coins of the Hellenistic kingdom. In these portraits, Alexander was shown with the horns of Ammon sprouting from his temples as a sign of his divinity. Gradually, the idea of portraying a ruler in his or her lifetime became acceptable.

The Roman Republic preferred figures from mythology and female allegories of abstract ideas such as Concord, Abundance and Victory. Significantly, Julius Caesar, who had ambitions to become the greatest Roman of them all, was the first to be depicted on coins during his lifetime. After Caesar was assasinated, Brutus issued silver denarii with his own portrait on the obverse. This coin was also an interesting early attempt to use coins as a propa-

ABOVE The obverse of a silver tetradrachm depicting the head of Alexander the Great, and (LEFT) the reverse showing a seated Athena with shield.

RIGHT Obverse of one of a beautiful series of coins issued by the Popes in 1694. It was struck on new the screw press.

ganda medium for the reverse shows the cap of Liberty between two daggers, with the inscription EID MAR, a none too subtle reference to the murder of Caesar in the name of liberty, on the Ides of March. Thereafter Roman coins were outstanding for the realism of their portraiture, usually done in profile and sometimes showing the royal lineage. When the Roman Empire in the West collapsed in the late fifth century, the coins of the Byzantium empire showed facing portraits of Christ and full-length portraits of rulers. The portraits were becoming stereotyped and less realistic.

BELOW Reverse of the above coin showing the figure of Plenty.

The Dark Ages

During the Dark Ages, the coins of Europe degenerated. The barbarian tribes who overran the empire struck coins on Roman models, but they lacked the skills and equipment to produce the same results.

The petty rulers of the Anglo-Saxon kingdoms, for example, might portray themselves with the laurels and togas of their Roman predecessors, but the results using the technique of engraving dies by means of "dot and squiggle" punches meant that some of the profiles are worse than caricature. Notable exceptions were the unique gold solidus of York, showing a facing bust of Archbishop Wigmund (837-54) and the silver pennies of Canterbury, showing Archbishop Ceolnoth (833-70). The facing portrait concept was revived by Edward the Confessor (1042-66) and continued by William the Conqueror. Though somewhat static and predictably idealized, the full-face portrait graced English coins until the beginning of the sixteenth century when engraver Alexander Brugsal depicted Henry VII as he really looked.

The rise of realism

In 1463, the Italian city state of Milan began issuing coins showing Duke Francesco I Sforza as he really was. Under his successor, Galeazzo-Maria Sforza, Milan adopted a silver lira (known first as a grossone, then testone) in 1474 and it is with this coin that modern coinage is said to have begun.

Louis XII of France struck portrait coins in 1500-12 in his capacity as Duke of Milan, and brought the idea back to France where the name was spelled *teston*. From France, realistic portraits spread to England and rapidly throughout Europe. The last immobilized portrait coins being the silver five sueldos of Majorca and Valentia in 1556. Since then portraits have become more and more realistic, even unflattering. Arguably the ugliest portrait is that found on Austrian *thalers* of

1682 showing the Archduke Leopold I whose distinctive Habsburg jaw was exceptionally exaggerated.

People must have thought that Britain had returned to the era of the immobilized, idealized portrait during the reign of Queen Victoria. As late as 1887, many coins depicted Queen Victoria as a teenager, although by that time she had reigned for half a century and was 68 years old!

*BELOW
Presidents
Washington to
Reagan surround
the Statue of
Liberty on the Isle
of Man crown
(1987).*

Full face versus profile?

For practical purposes, a profile is preferable to a full-face portrait. A profile relies mainly on the distinctive outline of the effigy for realism with other features being suggested with a few subtle lines that do not materially affect the height of the relief.

In modern coins, where the ability to stack neatly is a decided advantage, low relief is essential and this can only be achieved satisfactorily by means of a profile. In some modern coins, such as the current Dutch series, the profile has been reduced to a simple two-dimensional silhouette.

A facing bust, on the other hand, generally requires a fairly high relief to show the distinctive features. After the wretched "Coppernoses" (see page 18) facing busts were never again used in Britain, though they have been elsewhere in recent times.

Both the Cayman Islands and the Isle of Man issued coins in 1974, with facing portraits of Winston Churchill to celebrate the centenary of his birth, and in 1977 the Cayman Islands marked the Silver Jubilee of Queen Elizabeth II by issuing a set of five dollar-sized coins, portraying the queens regnant from Mary I to Victoria. An even more ambitious series of 1980 featured monarchs from Edward the Confessor to the present day monarch, most depicted in facing busts.

ABOVE Facing portrait of Sir Winston Churchill.

Side-by-side facing portraits of Prince Charles and Lady Diana Spencer appeared on gold coins in 1981 celebrating the royal wedding. The Isle of Man has had some very striking silver crowns portraying Prince Philip and the disabled air-ace Sir Douglas Bader, while a crown of 1987 bore a stunning array of American presidents from George Washington to Ronald Reagan.

ABOVE Simple portrait of Queen Beatrix.

The late Emperor Hirohito of Japan appeared full-face on coins of Liberia, while many of the crowns of recent years, in honor of Queen Elizabeth the Queen Mother, have portrayed her full-face.

ABOVE Young head of Queen Victoria, and (BELOW) the Jubilee head on the obverse of sixpences.

NONE BUT THE DEAD

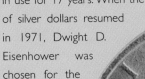

Kings and queens, emperors and empresses, princes, dukes and presidents have graced the coins of many countries, but the United States has a rule that no living person should be portrayed on a coin. George Washington resolutely refused to allow his image to appear on a coin when he became the first president on the grounds that it smacked of monarchy and was totally out of place and not in keeping with republic sentiments.

ABOVE Franklin D. Roosevelt (ten cent).

As far as the general circulating coinage is concerned, this convention began with the cent in 1909 when a bust of Abraham Lincoln replaced the head of an Indian chief. This was intended as a mark of respect at the time of Lincoln's birth centenary, but has remained since.

ABOVE John F. Kennedy (50 cent).

In 1932, Washington was placed on the quarter dollar followed by Thomas Jefferson on the nickel (1938) and Benjamin Franklin on the half dollar (1948).

Franklin Delano Roosevelt died in 1945 and as a tribute to his presidency, his portrait was placed on the dimes minted from 1946 onwards. Similarly, John F. Kennedy appeared on the half dollar in 1964, shortly after his assassination — notwithstanding a federal law that stated that the design of a coin must remain unchanged for at least 25 years, and the Franklin design had only been in use for 17 years. When the minting of silver dollars resumed in 1971, Dwight D. Eisenhower was chosen for the obverse.

ABOVE Abraham Lincoln (one cent).

ABOVE Thomas Jefferson (five cent).

ABOVE Dwight Eisenhower (one dollar).

Coins out of time

Sometimes the portraits on coins are at odds with the prevailing political situation. Philip II of Spain was portrayed on coins of the Netherlands up to 1581, although this region of his realm had been in revolt since 1577. Charles I continued to appear on English coins despite the fact that the Tower Mint was controlled by parliament during the Civil War. In France, the image of Louis XIV prevailed on coins after the revolution broke out in 1789, although there was a subtle change in his title to "King of the French" rather than "King of France". Only after he lost his head under the guillotine was his effigy dropped and replaced with various allegorical motifs inspired by classical art.

ABOVE Allegorical head on this Colombian coin of 1967.

ABOVE Greek coin with detailed figurehead.

years, Arab rulers have also breached the ban with portraits being found on coins of Iraq (since 1931), Libya (1952), Kuwait (1976), Morocco (since 1956), Tunisia (since 1965), the United Arab Emirates (since 1964) and Jordan (since 1968).

Muslim law

The earliest Islamic coins were closely modelled on their Byzantine or Sassanian contemporaries; but in 76 A.D. the Khalif Abd al-Malik banned the use of portraits, in compliance with a rule of the Prophet Muhammad who prohibited the making of representations of living things. This ban persists to this day, although it was ignored by the Emporer Jahangir, who contrived to break the Muslim ban on alcohol as well; his mohurs of 1611-14 showed him holding a cup of wine! From the beginning of this century the Shahs of Persia ignored the Islamic ban and placed their effigies on many coins. In recent

ABOVE Prohibited portrait on a United Arab Emirates coin.

ABOVE Austrian shilling with allegorical motif.

Two-faced coins

Coins bearing two portraits face-to-face are said to be vis-à-vis or bajoire (from the French baiser, to kiss). Some Roman coins have this feature, but it was never popular. Nero issued an aureus in 54 A.D. with confronted busts of himself and his mother, Agrippina, portrayed as if they were the same age. It was only in the fifteenth century, when the greater availability of silver permitted larger coins that face-to-face portraits came into their own. Ferdinand of Aragon and Isabella of Castile set the trend with the excelente of 1497, which symbolized the union of two jointly-ruling monarchs.

LEFT Conjoined portraits of William III and Mary on a silver half-crown (1693).

Full-face portraits side-by-side have seldom been used, mainly because it is difficult to produce even one realistic facing bust portrait on a coin. In classical times, however, it was a popular device, especially among the Byzantines whose coins portrayed the emperor and empress on the obverse, with two or more of their ancestors on the reverse.

ABOVE Jugate profiles on a Thai coin.

By far the most usual practice of portraying two or more persons is to show them side-by-side, one slightly overlapping the other. Such portraits are said to be jugate (from the Latin meaning "yoked together") or conjoined. Jugate profiles may be found on classical coins from around 282-203 B.C. through to extensive issues of the Roman emperors. Jugate profiles made a comeback in the sixteenth century, as portraiture in general became more realistic. It became very fashionable in German principalities where brothers ruled jointly. A jugate device was used for coinage portrait of Charles and Diana in 1981.

LEFT The reverse of the crown issued in 1981 to celebrate a royal marriage.

ABOVE The reverse of the William III and Mary coin with interlocking initials.

45

ABOVE *One of the Ireland's "Barnyard" series.*

ABOVE *"Barnyard" coin sculptured by Percy Metcalfe.*

Pictorialism

Although symbols and heraldry continue to dominate coin design, there has been a resurgence of pictorialism in recent years. Not since classical times have everyday, circulating coins presented such a picture gallery in miniature.

ABOVE
"Monticello" on the reverse of a five cent coin.

The United States broke new ground in 1913 when James Earl Fraser designed a nickel with the head of an Indian chief on the obverse and a buffalo on the reverse. The Jefferson nickel, which superseded it in 1938, showed Jefferson's mansion, Monticello, on the reverse, and in 1959 the Lincoln cent came into line by featuring the Lincoln Memorial on its reverse. The Franklin half dollar featured the Liberty bell, while the Eisenhower dollar showed an eagle – the emblem of the Apollo XI mission – landing on the moon.

In 1928, the Irish Free State replaced British coins with its own distinctive series. The harp of Ireland appeared on the obverse, but each reverse featured animals and birds. The "Barnyard" series, as it was known to collectors, broke new ground in realism and simplicity. The fashion for pictorial motifs spread to the

United Kingdom and in 1937 a wren (farthing), Sir Francis Drake's ship "Golden Hind" (halfpenny) and a thrift plant (nickel-brass threepence) appeared on some denominations.

In 1938-9, Australia adopted a similar policy, introducing the kangaroo, ears of wheat and merino ram. Canada began using pictorial reverses in 1935 when a dollar showing voyageurs in a canoe was introduced. This was followed by lower denominations showing maple leaves, a beaver, the schooner "Bluenose" and a caribou.

Nowadays, many countries use the reverse of their coins to depict scenery and landmarks, fauna and flora, or aspects of industry and commerce. More than ever before, coins have become a vital medium, for projecting a country's image as well as furnishing attractive souvenirs for tourists and visitors.

ABOVE *Pictorial reverse of the Lincoln Memorial on a one cent.*

ABOVE *"The eagle has landed" one dollar coin.*

ABOVE The "Barnyard" series
was retained on decimal coins.

ABOVE Wren on a
United Kingdom farthing.

ABOVE The maple leaf
of Canada.

ABOVE Thrift plant
threepence (1952).

ABOVE "Barnyard"
antics in Ireland.

ABOVE Canada's
caribou on a quarter.

ABOVE Merino ram on
an Australian shilling.

ABOVE "Bluenose" on
Canadian ten cent coin.

ABOVE A beaver coins
it in for Canada.

Reverse motifs

The Greek custom of featuring an attribute of a deity on the reverse had its counterpart in the allegorical designs on Roman coins. Because the Romans regarded coins as all important propaganda medium, the reverse designs were frequently changed. Not only did they symbolize Justice, Concord, Victory, Abundance and other abstract ideas, they, frequently depicted great public works.

In the Dark Ages, coin reverses degenerated. In the Byzantine Empire, a cross, a symbol of Christianity, was a very popular device and this was copied in Western Europe in medieval times. Not only did this serve as a Christian emblem, it provided a convenient guide when

cutting coins into halves and quarters for use as small change. The cross was the dominant feature of English silver coins until the seventeenth century, although latterly it was often superimposed on a heraldic shield. A similar pattern existed elsewhere in Europe; the obverse bore the ruler's portrait while the reverse showed a Christian symbol, and latterly a State emblem.

National symbols continue to provide the main fare for coin reverses. Thus the current British decimal coins show, for example, a crowned portcullis, the triple plumes of the Prince of Wales and the seated figure of Britannia. When the pound coins were introduced in 1983, it was decided to place the English royal arms on the reverse, but in each succeeding year a different heraldic motif has been used.

RIGHT A proof set of the United Kingdom decimal coinage (1972) with the Royal Silver Wedding coin and the Mint's bronze plaquette.

CHAPTER FIVE

DATES, LEGENDS AND INSCRIPTIONS

• • • •

The first English dated coin was issued by Edward VI in 1548, with the date in Roman numerals rendered in Gothic script. Three years later, the first silver crown bore the date – 1551 – in Arabic numerals. Dating coins did not become common in Europe until the seventeenth century.

Earlier coins could be dated approximately from the sequence marks denoting Trials of the Pyx. Alternatively, a reference might be made to a regnal year, with the Latin formula ANNO REGNI (in the year of our reign) followed by Roman numerals.

Until the fifteenth century, coins of the Islamic countries compensated for their lack of portraiture or pictorialism by having lengthy inscriptions and the day, month and year of issue rendered in words. Such precision was virtually unheard of in European coins.

In the United States, federal law requires coins to bear the year in which they are actually struck, while in other countries, coins bear the year in which they were first struck. Sometimes a compromize is effected as in the "dot" coins of Canada. The same thing happened in 1948 when coins dated 1947 were struck with a tiny maple leaf alongside the date.

From 1868 to 1982 most Spanish coins bore two dates – the larger was the year of authorization, while the year of minting was denoted by way of a six-pointed star on which a minuscule date was inscribed incuse.

Occasionally the last digit on a coinage die is altered to a later date merely by striking over it with a numeral punch. Coins minted from amended dies are termed overstrikes or overdates and many instances have been recorded in both British and American coinage of the nineteenth century.

ABOVE Obverse of the 1858 Victorian copper penny of the United Kingdom.

Legends and inscriptions

Collectors reserve the term "legend" for any lettering that runs round the perimeter of a coin, and "inscription" for lettering that runs across the surface in a straight line. Conversely, lettering inscribed on the edge of the coin is known as an edge inscription.

The earliest Greek coins bore no lettering and are said to be anepigraphic; their identity can only be deduced by the devices stamped on them. Athenian coins were instantly recognizable by the head of Athena and her owl, while Pegasus indicated Corinth, a turtle Aegina,

and a boy on a dolphin Tarentum. A notable exception to this, however, was the electrum stater of Miletus in Ionia, which featured a stag and was inscribed in Greek "I am the badge of Phanes", this otherwise unrecorded individual having been the magistrate during whose period of office the coin was struck. Otherwise, only the occasional cryptic letter was used. For example, a capital *theta* on coins of Phocaea and the ancient Q-shaped letter *koppa* on coins of Corinth. By the sixth century B.C., however, Athenian coins were being inscribed ATHE, and in the fifth century other city-states were following suit.

The earliest inscriptions were rather haphazardly placed on the reverse, often consisting of groups of two or three letters at the top and bottom. By the fourth century, legends were appearing around the perimeter and this pattern has been standard ever since. Many of the coins from the Hellenistic kingdoms had very long and elaborate inscriptions, reciting the name and titles of the ruler. To accommodate them the lettering appeared in straight lines, arranged like a

square with the reverse motif in the middle. The Seleucids and Bactrians even had to resort to double-banking their inscriptions, one square within the other.

Roman inscriptions

It never seems to have occurred to the Greeks and their successors to spread the inscription to the obverse, that was left to the Romans. By the first century B.C. rudimentary legends were appearing on the obverse, but reverse inscriptions were confined to the exergue. This is the segment at the foot of the reverse, divided from rest of the field by a straight line. The British gold sovereign has the date in the exergue, while the current 50 pence coin has the numerals of value in this position.

In the last years of the Roman Republic, legends on both sides became longer, culminating in the coins of Octavian, which bore the legend DIVI IVLI F. (son of the divine Julius). The titles on Roman coins included such abbreviations as TRP (*tribunicia potestas*), PM (*pontifex maximus*) and cos (*consul*). This was followed by Roman numerals which indicate a year of the emperor's reign.

Cryptic inscriptions

Many of the inscriptions on Roman coins are cryptic, being confined to a abbreviations and initials, as are the inscriptions on coins of the German states of the seventeenth and eighteenth centuries. This system spread to Britain under George I and his successors. On the obverse, the king's name was followed by D.G. M. BR. FR. ET HIB. REX F.D. This stood for the Latin legend *Dei Gratia Magnae Britanniae, Franciae et Hiberniae Rex, Fidei Defensor* – "By the Grace of God, King of Great Britain, France and Ireland, Defender of the Faith".

ABOVE Reverse of a George III shilling showing the abbreviations of his titles.

LEFT The boy on the dolphin graces the coins of Tarentum. This coin dates from the fifth century.

Mint-marks

As governments everywhere became more centralized at the end of the Middle Ages, the numbers of mints fell rapidly. Even where two or more mints continued to operate, their coins were no longer identified by the name and location of the mint and moneyers' names. The last English coins to bear a town name were the pennies of Philip II of Spain and Mary Tudor (1554–8). Thereafter, the place of striking was denoted by an initial letter or a symbol. These are known as mint-marks and appear on many current coins.

ABOVE The D (top center) indicates the Munich mint.

ABOVE G (left of the 2) means Karlsruhe.

Modern British coins do not have a mint-mark if they are struck by the Royal Mint, but some bronze coins with an "H" beside the date were struck by Ralph Heaton of Birmingham, while others lettered KN were produced at King's Norton, in Birming-ham. The Birmingham Mint still uses an "H" as a mint-mark on overseas coins. Coins with the letters PM denote the Pobjoy Mint of Sutton, Surrey.

France and Germany adopted a system of denoting individual mints by means of letters of the alphabet. Thus a French coin lettered A would have been struck at Paris, whereas C denoted Castelsarrasin and W Lille. At the present time, all coins are struck at the French Mint near Paris.

Germany, however, continues to use several mints, and their coins may be recognized by these letters: A (Berlin), D (Munich), F (Stuttgart), G (Karlsruhe) and J (Hamburg).

Until recently, coins struck at the United States Mint in Philadelphia were unmarked, but the letter P now denotes certain issues. The branch mints, on the other hand, are, or were, denoted by initial letters such as C (Charlotte), CC (Carson City), D (Dahlonega or Denver), O (New Orleans) S (San Francisco) and W (West Point).

The following system was used to distinguish gold sovereigns and half sovereigns struck at various mints: Sydney (S), Melbourne (M) and Perth (P); and at Ottawa, Canada (C), Calcutta, India (I) and Pretoria, South Africa (SA).

Difference or sequence marks

Mint-mark is also loosely used to denote a letter or symbol that ought more properly to be known as a difference mark or a sequence mark. In England, these marks were associated with the Trial of the Pyx, a ceremonial testing of the purity and weight of certain gold and silver coins set aside in pyxis, special boxes. The symbols that appeared on coins denoted a period between each trial, and as these trials were held annually they help date hammered coinage before 1662. The symbols appeared on both the obverse and reverse, at the beginning of the legend (about one o'clock). It is interesting to note that, in 1983, the Royal Mint revived a mark of this sort, in the form of a long cross *fitchée*, to indicate the beginning of the incuse edge inscription on pound coins.

BELOW The five franc of 1843 showing Marques et Différents. Lamb and flag (left) the privy mark of mint director; the B (right) the mint-mark for Rouen; and the dog's head (center) the privy mark of the Engraver-General.

BELOW This bronze penny of King George V (1919) was minted at the Heaton Mint, Birmingham. Note, the H just to the left of the date.

53

Privy marks

French coins bear two symbols, known to collectors as privy marks, although the official term in France is Marques et Différents. These represent the men responsible for the dies. One series denotes the Engraver General (or, since 1880, the Chief Engraver), while the other denotes the director of each mint. The engravers' marks are common to all coins, as the dies were supplied from one central authority. In the past century, these marks have consisted of fasces (1880-96), torch (1896-1930), wing (1931-58), owl (1958-74) and fish (since 1974). The directors' marks vary from mint to mint. The bee (symbol of the Bonaparte family) appeared on Parisian coins from 1861 to 1879, but during the Commune of 1871 the mint was under the control of Citizen Camélinat, whose privy mark was a trident. From 1880 the symbol represented the office and therefore only a cornucopia has been used since.

The term privy mark is also used at the present time for symbols added to the design of a definitive coin of a permanent series in order to convert it into a commemorative piece. A good examples of this is the Manx coin with a baby's crib to commemorate the birth of Prince William (1982).

Provenance marks

Provenance marks are letters or symbols that identify the source of the metal. The best-known examples of this in British coinage are the gold and silver of 1703, with the word VIGO below Queen Anne's bust, and the coins of George II dated 1745-6, inscribed LIMA. Such

BELOW Isle of Man five pence (1979) showing the Millennium privy-mark.

RIGHT Roses and plumes indicate the provenance of the Company for Smelting Pit Coale and Sea Coale on this half-crown of 1712.

and having interlinked CC in alternate quadrants (reverse) denoted silver from the Welsh Copper Company. Silver coins with English roses and Welsh plumes on the reverse indicated bullion supplied by the Company for Smelting Pit Coale and Sea Coale. Gold coins of George II, were produced from metal supplied by the East India Company and bore the initials E.I.C.

LEFT Note the S.C.C. (South Sea Company) initials between the heraldic shields on this half-crown of 1723.

BELOW Below James II's neck is the badge of the Africa Company that supplied the bullion.

coins were struck from Spanish bullion seized by an Anglo-Dutch expedition to Vigo Bay in 1702, and by Admiral Anson during his round-the-world voyage of 1740-4.

Bullion from the Guinea coast, supplied by the Africa Company, was denoted by an elephant or an elephant and castle (1663-1722). Silver coins of George I inscribed S.S.C. came from bullion of the South Sea Company that when bust in 1720, while coins inscribed W.C.C. below the king's neck (obverse)

55

Control marks

Control marks are sometimes used to denote the particular ingots from which the coin blanks were cut. This system, using letters or numerals, goes back to 265 B.C. when Egyptian silver didrachms were thus marked. This practice was used in Athens (second and first centuries B.C.) and on the coins of the Roman Republic. It has its modern counterpart in the British gold and silver coins of 1863-80, which have tiny numerals on the reverse, identifying the die used.

In recent years, many coins of the Isle of Man and Gibraltar have had security die marks in the form of two capital letters discreetly concealed in the design. Early in 1937, Canada issued the "dot" coins in which a dot below the wreath distinguished emergency issue coins. Of the 678,823 cents struck, only eight were issued, while of the 192,194 dimes struck, only four are believed to be in existence.

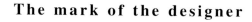

The mark of the designer

In many cases, the name or initials of the designer or die engraver may also be found somewhere on the obverse or reverse, or even on both sides. This tradition goes back to the fifth century B.C. when certain large coins of Syracuse bore the abbreviated names of their engravers, Kimon and Euainetos.

Many French coins bear the engraver's name or signature in full, but in the circulating coins of the United Kingdom the only man to have this honor was Benedetto Pistrucci, denoted by B.P. Hitherto, engravers and designers were not identified, but since then many artists have been denoted For example, W.W. for William Wyon. During the present reign, eight different sets of designers' initials have been used, but at least six other designers have remained anonymous.

CHAPTER SIX

THE COIN COLLECTOR'S GUIDE

• • • •

Coin collecting is a satisfying hobby that can be tailored to suit anyone's purse. In fact, anyone's purse may, at any given time, contain the nucleus of a collection!

You can restrict your interests to current coins of your own country, collecting different dates and looking out for die variations in each denomination; or you can collect the coins of countries visited on business or vacation. The drawbacks of these approaches are that you will end up with a diverse collection and many of your specimens may not be in mint condition. You may decide to collect coins in a certain metal, or concentrate on coins of a specific size. There are collectors who restrict their interest to minor coins. More pictorial coin design has encouraged collecting along thematic lines — fauna and flora, historic events and personalities, buildings, or means of travel.

BELOW A thematic coin collection based on architecture. These coins come from Iceland, Macau, Malaysia, Indonesia and Thailand.

Condition

BELOW An engraving (1693) of numismatics in front of a baroque coin cabinet.

Condition is by far the most important factor in determining the value of a coin. Beginners are surprised to discover the differential that exists between a coin in flawless condition and one showing marks of circulation.

Normally, the condition factor must be taken in conjunction with the degree of scarcity. Although Roman coins exist in Extremely Fine condition, the collector in this field will generally have to lower his or her sights or give up collecting. For modern coins, however, the condition of a coin is paramount. Of course there are great rarities, such as the 1952 half crown, the only known example of which had obviously been in circulation for years before it was spotted. But modern coins, especially those that are still current, should not be collected unless they are in perfect condition.

Because of the highly mechanized nature of coin production, it is virtually impossible to obtain a freshly minted circulating coin in absolutely perfect condition, but when it comes to proofs and coins packaged as uncirculated specimens, you have a right to expect the best. Even when fresh from the mint, coins will be found to have minute edge knocks and blemishes caused as they tumble from the press and are bagged up.

The grading system

Apart from proofs, the various grades of condition that the collector will encounter in auction catalogs and dealers' lists are as follows:

Fleur de coin (usually abbreviated to FDC) is synonymous with the American expression BU.

Brilliant Uncirculated (BU or B. Unc.) usually describes only modern proof coins.

Old coins

Uncirculated (Unc.) is the highest grade normally applied to a coin struck by standard mint machinery. A bronze penny, in this grade should possess the brilliant copper-red luster that distinguishes a newly minted coin. With age, this tends to darken attractively, as the coin acquires a patina. This is caused by atmospheric oxidation and is, in fact, a protective rust.

It must be stressed that on no account should any attempt be made to remove the patina by polishing or abrasion. Such action is little short of vandalism and would effectively destroy the numismatic value of a coin. In uncirculated coins, even the most delicate hairlines should be sharply defined.

Extremely Fine (EF) denotes a coin that is in a state of almost pristine perfection, but has been handled to some degree. It should have every detail of the engraving clearly delineated, but will probably have lost some of its original luster.

Very Fine (VF) coins will have slight traces of wear on their highest surfaces. Points to watch for are the fine lines in the hair of the portrait or signs of wear on the truncation of the bust, the highest point of the obverse. Coins in VF condition are collectable only if no better specimens are easily obtainable.

Collectors are sometimes tempted to buy coins in this, or lower, condition in order to fill gaps, but as VF coins will never have the resale potential of the higher grades, such purchases are often false economy.

Below VF, coins are not really worth considering unless they are scarce. Dealers do not usually handle modern items in the lower grades unless they are rare; however, the following definitions may be useful where older coins are concerned:

Fine (F) describes a coin in worn condition where higher points are worn smooth and the lettering has become thicker and coarser.

Very Good (VG) describes a coin where only a small fraction of the finer detail has survived while high relief and lettering will be quite blurred.

Good (G) indicates that a coin that is worn smooth all over with a date just readable. Below this grade comes Fair, Mediocre and Poor. These terms have now become virtually synonymous, although "Poor" usually refers to coins that are clipped or pierced as well as worn.

ABOVE AND BELOW Ships have long been a popular coin theme.

Fine distinctions

The grades listed on the previous page do not in themselves permit of the subtle, almost imperceptible, shading from one into the others, so it is sometimes necessary to modify them. Thus between FDC and EF one might find "Nearly FDC" and "Good EF", while in the United States collectors use such expressions as "About Uncirculated" (AU) and "EF Plus".

Where one side of the coin is better than the other, an oblique stroke between two grades (for example, F/VF) indicates that the obverse is Fine while the reverse is Very Fine.

"Slabbing"

Many of the trends in coin collecting have their origins in the United States and the principles of "slabbing" are now widely employed. Basically, this entails the precise grading of coins by an accredited dealer who then "slabs" or encapsulates the coin in a small transparent folder that permits the details of the coin, including its grade, to be entered. The system, perfected by the American Numismatic Association, is now so precise as to have rendered the gradings used in Britain and Europe obsolete.

American collectors now divide proofs into five distinct grades: Proof-70 (Perfect Proof), Proof-67 (Gem Proof), Proof-65 (Choice Proof), Proof-63 (Select Proof) and Proof-60 (Proof).

Uncirculated coins are graded into the same five categories, with MS (Mint State) prefixing a number: MS-70 (Perfect), MS-67 (Gem), MS-65 (Choice), MS-63 (Select) and MS-60 (Uncirculated).

Below 60, numbers 1–59 have been employed to indicate the various degrees of wear: Choice About Uncirculated (AU-55), About Uncirculated (AU50), Choice Extremely Fine (EF-45), Extremely Fine (EF-40), Choice Very Fine (VF-30), Very Fine (VF-20), Fine (F-12), Very Good (VG-8), Good (G-4), About Good (AG-4) and Basal State (BS-1). Time spent mastering and understanding these grades and their implications on your collection, is time well-spent.

THIS PAGE Many coins depict animals, and many collectors hunt them down.

THE NEED TO SPECIALIZE

Sooner or later you will find that if you are going to make any headway with your hobby you will have to specialize. To a large extent your choice of subject will depend on the amount of money you want to spend, but personal preferences are also important and a surprising range of different aspects of numismatics can be tailored to suit your tastes and pocket.

One area for specialization would be the early coins of the West Indies. The romance of pirates, buccaneers and swashbuckling on the Spanish Main is reflected in the array of coins shown here. Many coins from Europe circulated in the Caribbean, but were countermarked with new values and insignia to denote local usage.

Small change was created in two ways. A large coin was cut into smaller pieces such as halves, quarters and tiny segments, or the center was punched out and both the central plug and outer ring were countermarked for use as coins of different denominations. A long "bit" was 15 cents and a short "bit" ten cents. From these practices came the American expression "two bits" (25 cents), and the *bit* which was the unit of currency (1904-17) in the Danish West Indies.

THIS PAGE Coins that are literally a jig-saw puzzle of history and human adventure.

Care and storage

*RIGHT Coin cases
will keep your
collection in good
condition while
travelling or for
more permanent
storage.*

There is no point in going to a great deal of trouble and expense in selecting the best coins you can afford, only to let them deteriorate by neglect and mishandling. Housing coins is the biggest problem of all, so it is important to give a lot of attention to this.

Coins are best stored at average room temperature and humidity, so it is advisable to place small bags of silica gel crystals in the cabinets or boxes to combat atmospheric moisture. These crystals absorb water from the atmosphere, turning from blue to pink in the process. The ideal, but most expensive, method is the coin cabinet, constructed of air-dried mahogany, walnut or rosewood (never oak, cedar or any highly-resinous timber likely to cause chemical tarnish). These cabinets

*RIGHT A coin
cabinet that will
exclude dust and
atmospheric
pollution.*

have banks of shallow drawers containing trays made of the same wood, with half-drilled holes of various sizes to cater for the different denominations of coins.

An excellent compromise are coin trays in durable, felt-lined materials with shallow compartments to suit various sizes of coin. The trays interlock so that they build up into a cabinet of the desired size. An alternative is a drawer-stacking system with clear glass trays that fit into standard bookshelves.

There are also various storage systems which operate on the principle of narrow drawers in which the coins are stored in envelopes of chemically-inert plastic. A strip across the top holds a little slip giving a brief description, catalog number and the price of each coin. The traditional method used by many collectors was to house coins in small, air-dried manila envelopes that could be stored in narrow wooden or stout card boxes.

One Australian museum satisfactorily keeps its coins in manila envelopes stored in plastic lunch-boxes

Cleaning your collection

Cleaning coins is something that should never be undertaken lightly; indeed, it is better not to attempt it than risk irreparable damage.

Coins should always be handled with care, by holding the rims between forefinger and thumb. The acids and oils secreted by the fingers can leave indelible fingerprints on coins, so wear a pair of fine silk or cotton gloves while handling coins. Warm water containing a mild detergent will work wonders in removing surface dirt and grease from most coins, but silver is best washed in a decinormal solution of ammonia and warm water, while gold coins can be cleaned with dilute citric acid (such as lemon Juice). Copper or bronze coins present more of a problem, but patches of verdigris can usually be removed by careful washing in a 20 per cent solution of sodium sesquicarbonate. War-time coins made of tin, zinc, iron or steel can be cleaned in a five per cent solution of caustic soda containing some aluminium or zinc foil or filings, but they must be rinsed afterwards in clean water and dried.

If cleaning should only be approached with the greatest trepidation, polishing is definitely out! Polishing a coin may improve its superficial appearance for a few days, but the abrasive action will destroy the patina and reduce the fineness of the high points of its surface.

LEFT Handle your coins by the rim using forefinger and thumb.

DEALERS AND AUCTIONEERS

The numismatic trade has been around for centuries and arose as a sideline of goldsmiths and bankers. Spink & Son of England claimed to have been established in 1722, as their billhead of 1897 illustrates, but when historians were researching the firm's history for its bicentenary they discovered to their astonishment that it had actually been in existence since the Restoration of Charles II in 1660. William S. Lincoln of New Oxford Street in London was one of the leading dealers at the turn of the century, trading in postage stamps and crests, as well as coins and medals.

In an era before photographic illustrations were possible, reproductions of coins appeared as line drawings and in many cases these were much clearer than the actual photographs that later superseded them! By the nineteenth century, London had become the center of the world coin trade, and to this day it remains the headquarters of the leading auctioneers in this particular field.

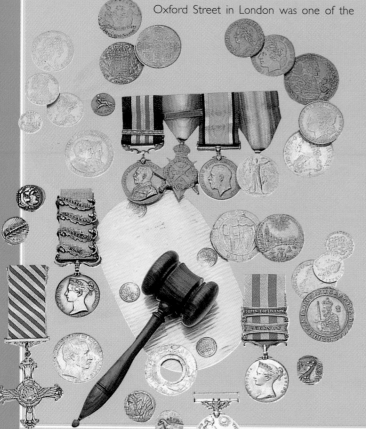

RIGHT Coin collecting is history within history as this brochure and bill of sale show.

LEFT The path of the coin collector is bound to cross that of the medallist.